Contents

21st Century

1) Who was Chelsea manager at the start of the 21st century?

2) In what year did Gianfranco Zola leave the club in order to sign for Cagliari?

3) Who became the first Peruvian to appear for the club after signing in 2007?

4) Who became Chelsea's youngster ever player when he appeared as a substitute against Macclesfield Town in the FA Cup in 2007?

5) How old was Didier Drogba when he scored his final goal for Chelsea?

6) What squad number has Cesar Azpilicueta worn since he arrived at Chelsea?

7) In which two seasons did Didier Drogba win the Premier League Golden Boot award?

8) Which Chelsea player won the PFA Players' Player of the Year award for the 2016/17 Premier League season?

9) In what year did Ashley Cole move from Arsenal to Chelsea?

10) When Chelsea dented Liverpool's title hopes by winning 2-0 at Anfield in 2014, which future Liverpool player was in the Chelsea side?

11) Who became permanent club captain after John Terry left the club in 2017?

12) Who scored an own goal against Chelsea in February 2019 as Tottenham went down to a 2-0 defeat at Stamford Bridge?

13) In what year did Fernando Torres notoriously miss an open goal against Manchester United at Old Trafford?

14) Which coach took charge of the 3-1 victory over Sunderland in December 2015 after Jose Mourinho left the club for the second time?

15) Christian Pulisic scored a hat-trick away from home against which team in October 2019?

16) In the 2004/05 Premier League season Chelsea broke the record for fewest goals conceded, how many goals did they let in during the campaign?

17) In what year did Luiz Felipe Scolari leave his role as Chelsea manager?

18) In the October 2006 match with Reading, both Petr Cech and Carlo Cudicini were stretchered off, leaving which player to play as goalkeeper for the remainder of the game?

19) Which young player won the man of the match award on his Premier League debut versus Everton in March 2020?

20) Which goalkeeper made his only Premier League start versus Newcastle on the last day of the 2005/06 season?

21) Who took over as manager when Carlo Ancelotti left the club in 2011?

Transfers I

1) Which striker arrived from Atletico Madrid in June 2000?

2) From which English club did Chelsea sign Eidur Gudjohnsen in June 2000?

3) Which goalkeeper signed on a free from Manchester United in January 2001?

4) Dan Petrescu was sold to which team in July 2000?

5) Which two players were signed from Barcelona in the summer of 2001?

6) Dennis Wise left the club in 2001 to join which English side?

7) Which midfielder was purchased from Manchester United in August 2003?

8) Arjen Robben and Alex were signed from which Dutch club in July 2004?

9) Which striker was bought from Marseille in July 2004?

10) Which side did Adrian Mutu sign for after leaving Chelsea in 2005?

11) Michael Essien arrived in August 2005 from which French team?

12) Which midfielder was signed on a free from Reading in 2007?

13) Which striker signed for Inter Milan after leaving Chelsea in August 2006?

14) From which club did Chelsea buy Nicolas Anelka in 2008?

15) Arjen Robben was sold to which team in 2007?

16) Which two players left Chelsea to join Manchester City in the summer of 2008?

17) Which winger arrived on loan from Inter Milan in February 2009?

18) Which goalkeeper signed on a free from Middlesbrough in July 2009?

19) Which defender was bought from Benfica in January 2011?

20) From which club was goalkeeper Thibaut Courtois signed in 2011?

21) Which striker was sold to Wigan Athletic in August 2010?

First Goals I – Name the clubs that these players scored their first goal for Chelsea against

1) Didier Drogba

2) John Terry

3) Frank Lampard

4) Fernando Torres

5) Ashley Cole

6) Daniel Sturridge

7) Nicolas Anelka

8) Michael Ballack

9) Ricardo Carvalho

10) Damien Duff

11) Arjen Robben

12) Jimmy-Floyd Hasselbaink

13) Alvaro Morata

Red Cards

1) Both Gary Cahill and Cesc Fabregas were sent off in an opening day defeat to which side in August 2017?

2) Chelsea lost 1-0 to Newcastle in the FA Cup in February 2005, which player finished the game in goal for the blues after Carlo Cudicini was dismissed?

3) John Terry missed the 2012 Champions League Final after being sent off in the Semi Final against Barcelona for kneeing which player?

4) Jose Bosingwa and which other player were sent off against QPR in the 1-0 loss in October 2011?

5) Thibaut Courtois was sent off during the 2-2 draw with which team in August 2015?

6) Which winger was sent off against West Brom in March 2006?

7) Chelsea lost 1-0 away to Aston Villa in March 2014, which two Chelsea players were dismissed?

8) Chelsea lost a tempestuous encounter with Manchester City in February 2010, which two Chelsea players were sent off as they went down to a 4-2 defeat?

9) Branislav Ivanovic and Fernando Torres were both sent off in a 3-2 defeat to which side in October 2012?

10) Frank Lampard was sent off for a foul on which Liverpool player in the February 2009 match between the two sides?

11) Jimmy-Floyd Hasselbaink was sent off against which team in September 2001, later seeing the red card rescinded?

12) Chelsea and Aston Villa played a thrilling match on Boxing day 2007 in which Ricardo Carvalho and Ashley Cole saw red, but what was the final score?

13) Chelsea beat Norwich on penalties in the FA Cup in 2018 despite having which two players sent off in extra time?

Memorable Goals

1) Who scored a stunning volley against West Ham in August 2000 after juggling the ball with his right foot and knee?

2) Who scored a spectacular overhead kick versus Leeds United in January 2003?

3) Didier Drogba won the Premier League goal of the month in October 2009 by rounding off a stunning team move versus which side?

4) Who was the unlikely winner of the Premier League goal of the month in January 2010 for his turn and finish versus Sunderland?

5) In what year did Michael Essien score a stunning long-range effort with the outside of his boot to secure a 1-1 draw with Arsenal?

6) Alex smashed in a long-range free kick against Arsenal in October 2010, who was in goal for the gunners?

7) Who scored the equaliser against Tottenham in May 2016 to end their title hopes and hand the Premier League title to Leicester City?

8) Chelsea drew 2-2 away against Barcelona to secure a place in the 2012 Champions League Final, who scored the first goal for the Blues on the night with a deft chip?

9) Who was in goal for Chelsea when Frank Lampard scored against his former side for Manchester City in September 2014?

10) Which midfielder stunned Old Trafford with a dipping effort from long-range against Manchester United in May 2005?

11) Who scored a winner deep into injury times to secure an opening day win against newly promoted Wigan Athletic in August 2005?

12) Claude Makelele scored his first Chelsea goal by converting a rebound from a missed penalty against which team in 2005?

13) Who scored the winning goal against Liverpool in 2003 to seal Champions League qualification?

14) Against which team did Frank Lampard score the goal to make him Chelsea's leading goal-scorer of all time?

Memorable Games

1) What was the score in Frank Lampard's first game as Chelsea manager, away to Manchester United in August 2019?

2) Who scored the winner in Jose Mourinho's first Premier League game as manager against Manchester United in August 2004?

3) Arsenal faced Chelsea in Arsene Wenger's 1000th game as manager, what was the score?

4) Who scored four goals as Chelsea beat Derby County 6-1 in March 2008?

5) Who was Chelsea manager when they thrashed Aston Villa 8-0 in December 2012?

6) Chelsea sealed the league title by tearing Wigan apart in an 8-0 win in May 2010, who was in goal for Wigan that day?

7) Manchester City beat Chelsea 6-0 in February 2019, who scored a hat-trick in the match?

8) What was the score-line when Chelsea beat Manchester City at home in the Premier League in October 2007?

9) Who made a superb last-minute save to claim a point for Chelsea during the dramatic 4-4 draw with Spurs in March 2008?

10) Which two players scored in the last 10 minutes to secure a 2-1 win away to Arsenal in December 2019?

11) Chelsea sealed the Premier League title with a 2-0 away win against which side in April 2005?

Transfers II

1) From where was Romelu Lukaku bought in 2011?

2) Who did Chelsea buy from Lille in June 2012?

3) Which player did Chelsea sign from Wigan Athletic in August 2012?

4) Which goalkeeper was signed from Fulham in 2013?

5) Which attacker was purchased from Basel in January 2014?

6) Chelsea sold which midfielder to Wolfsburg in January 2014?

7) Which two players were bought from Atletico Madrid in July 2014?

8) Didier Drogba re-signed for the club from where in 2014?

9) Which left back was sold to Sunderland in July 2014?

10) Chelsea sold which midfield player to Southampton in August 2015?

11) Which defender was bought from Fiorentina in August 2016?

12) Goalkeeper Asmir Begovic was sold to which English team in 2017?

13) Which former Premier League winning midfielder arrived from Leicester City in August 2017?

14) Which club did John Terry sign for after leaving Chelsea in 2017?

15) Striker Diego Costa was sold to which club in 2017?

16) Which former England goalkeeper signed for Chelsea in July 2018?

17) Jorginho was purchased from which club in July 2018?

18) Which team did Cesc Fabregas sign for in January 2019?

19) Mateo Kovacic arrived from which club in July 2019?

20) Which defender signed for Crystal Palace after leaving Chelsea in 2019?

Cup Games

1) Who scored from the penalty spot when Chelsea beat Manchester United 1-0 in the 2018 FA Cup Final?

2) Who infamously refused to be substituted during the 2019 League Cup Final?

3) Which lower league side beat Chelsea in the FA Cup fourth round in 2015?

4) How many FA cups did Ashley Cole win at Chelsea?

5) Who scored twice for Chelsea as they defeated Arsenal 2-1 in the 2007 League Cup Final?

6) Chelsea beat Everton 2-1 in the 2009 FA Cup Final, but who had put Everton ahead in the first minute?

7) In the FA Cup Semi Final against Newcastle in the year 2000, which player scored twice in the 2-1 win?

8) Chelsea won the last ever FA Cup Final to be staged at the old Wembley stadium in the year 2000, who scored the only goal as they defeated Aston Villa?

9) Which team beat Chelsea in the FA Cup in 2001, 2002, 2003 and 2004?

10) Who scored the winner in extra time to win the FA Cup for Chelsea versus Manchester United in 2007?

11) Chelsea beat Liverpool 3-2 after extra time to claim the 2005 League Cup trophy, which Liverpool player scored an own goal during normal time to equalise for the blues?

12) Which team did Chelsea hammer 7-0 in the Fa Cup third round in January 2011?

First Goals II

1) Diego Costa

2) Joe Cole

3) Scott Parker

4) David Luiz

5) Loic Remy

6) Michael Essien

7) Deco

8) Willian

9) Samuel Eto'o

10) Eden Hazard

11) Demba Ba

12) Mason Mount

13) Tammy Abraham

European Games

1) Chelsea beat Bayern Munich on penalties to win the Champions League Final in 2012, but who missed Chelsea's first spot kick in the shootout?

2) Who scored in stoppage time for Barcelona during the highly controversial Semi Final to knock Chelsea out of the Champions League in 2009?

3) Who scored the late winner as Chelsea knocked Arsenal out of the Champions League at the Quarter Final stage in 2004?

4) Chelsea knocked Liverpool out of the Champions League at the Quarter Final stage in 2009, but what was the aggregate score?

5) Which team did Chelsea lose to on penalties in the 2019 Super Cup after drawing 2-2 in normal time?

6) Who scored a late own goal as Liverpool drew 1-1 with Chelsea in the first leg of the Champions League Semi Final in 2008?

7) Who missed Chelsea's last penalty in the 2008 Champions League Final shoot-out to hand Manchester United the title?

8) When Chelsea faced Ajax in the group stage of the Champions League in November 2019 the Dutch side were reduced to 9 men, but what was the final score?

9) Which Chelsea player was sent off in the 2008 Champions League Final defeat to Manchester United?

10) Which team beat Chelsea in the Champions League Semi Final in 2004?

11) Who scored the injury time winner for Chelsea in the 2013 Europa League Final versus Benfica?

12) Which Swiss side knocked Chelsea out of the UEFA Cup at the First-Round stage in September 2000?

13) Chelsea lost in the UEFA Super Cup three times in the first 20 years of this century, which teams did they lose to?

21st Century Answers

1) Who was Chelsea manager at the start of the 21st century?
Gianluca Vialli

2) In what year did Gianfranco Zola leave the club in order to sign for Cagliari?
2003

3) Who became the first Peruvian to appear for the club after signing in 2007?
Claudio Pizarro

4) Who became Chelsea's youngster ever player when he appeared as a substitute against Macclesfield Town in the FA Cup in 2007?
Michael Woods

5) How old was Didier Drogba when he scored his final goal for Chelsea?
37

6) What squad number has Cesar Azpilicueta worn since he arrived at Chelsea?

28

7) In which two seasons did Didier Drogba win the Premier League Golden Boot award?

2006/07 and 2009/10

8) Which Chelsea player won the PFA Players' Player of the Year award for the 2016/17 Premier League season?

N'Golo Kante

9) In what year did Ashley Cole move from Arsenal to Chelsea?

2006

10) When Chelsea dented Liverpool's title hopes by winning 2-0 at Anfield in 2014, which future Liverpool player was in the Chelsea side?

Mo Salah

11) Who became permanent club captain after John Terry left the club in 2017?
Gary Cahill

12) Who scored an own goal against Chelsea in February 2019 as Tottenham went down to a 2-0 defeat at Stamford Bridge?
Kieran Trippier

13) In what year did Fernando Torres notoriously miss an open goal against Manchester United at Old Trafford?
2011

14) Which coach took charge of the 3-1 victory over Sunderland in December 2015 after Jose Mourinho left the club for the second time?
Steve Holland

15) Christian Pulisic scored a hat-trick away from home against which team in October 2019?
Burnley

16) In the 2004/05 Premier League season Chelsea broke the record for fewest goals conceded, how many goals did they let in during the campaign?
15

17) In what year did Luiz Felipe Scolari leave his role as Chelsea manager?
2009

18) In the October 2006 match with Reading, both Petr Cech and Carlo Cudicini were stretchered off, leaving which player to play as goalkeeper for the remainder of the game?
John Terry

19) Which young player won the man of the match award on his Premier League debut versus Everton in March 2020?
Billy Gilmour

20) Which goalkeeper made his only Premier League start versus Newcastle on the last day of the 2005/06 season?
Lenny Pidgeley

21) Who took over as manager when Carlo Ancelotti left the club in 2011?
Andre Villas-Boas

Transfers I Answers

1) Which striker arrived from Atletico
   Madrid in June 2000?
   Jimmy-Floyd Hasselbaink

2) From which English club did Chelsea
   sign Eidur Gudjohnsen in June 2000?
   Bolton Wanderers

3) Which goalkeeper signed on a free from
   Manchester United in January 2001?
   Mark Bosnich

4) Dan Petrescu was sold to which team in
   July 2000?
   Bradford City

5) Which two players were signed from
   Barcelona in the summer of 2001?
   **Emmanuel Petit and Boudewijn
   Zenden**

6) Dennis Wise left the club in 2001 to join which English side?
Leicester City

7) Which midfielder was purchased from Manchester United in August 2003?
Juan Sebastian Veron

8) Arjen Robben and Alex were signed from which Dutch club in July 2004?
PSV Eindhoven

9) Which striker was bought from Marseille in July 2004?
Didier Drogba

10) Which side did Adrian Mutu sign for after leaving Chelsea in 2005?
Juventus

11) Michael Essien arrived in August 2005 from which French team?
Lyon

12) Which midfielder was signed on a free from Reading in 2007?
Steve Sidwell

13) Which striker signed for Inter Milan after leaving Chelsea in August 2006?
Hernan Crespo

14) From which club did Chelsea buy Nicolas Anelka in 2008?
Bolton Wanderers

15) Arjen Robben was sold to which team in 2007?
Real Madrid

16) Which two players left Chelsea to join Manchester City in the summer of 2008?
Tal Ben-Haim and Shaun Wright-Phillips

17) Which winger arrived on loan from Inter Milan in February 2009?
Ricardo Quaresma

18) Which goalkeeper signed on a free from Middlesbrough in July 2009?
Ross Turnbull

19) Which defender was bought from Benfica in January 2011?
David Luiz

20) From which club was goalkeeper Thibaut Courtois signed in 2011?
Genk

21) Which striker was sold to Wigan Athletic in August 2010?
Franco Di Santo

First Goals I Answers

1) Didier Drogba
   Crystal Palace

2) John Terry
   Arsenal

3) Frank Lampard
   Levski Sofia

4) Fernando Torres
   West Ham

5) Ashley Cole
   West Ham

6) Daniel Sturridge
   Watford

7) Nicolas Anelka
   Wigan Athletic

8) Michael Ballack
   Werder Bremen

9) Ricardo Carvalho
   Real Betis

10) Damien Duff
    Wolverhampton Wanderers

11) Arjen Robben
    CSKA Moscow

12) Jimmy-Floyd Hasselbaink
    Manchester United

13) Alvaro Morata
    Burnley

Red Cards Answers

1) Both Gary Cahill and Cesc Fabregas were sent off in an opening day defeat to which side in August 2017?
Burnley

2) Chelsea lost 1-0 to Newcastle in the FA Cup in February 2005, which player finished the game in goal for the blues after Carlo Cudicini was dismissed?
Glen Johnson

3) John Terry missed the 2012 Champions League Final after being sent off in the Semi Final against Barcelona for kneeing which player?
Alexis Sanchez

4) Jose Bosingwa and which other player were sent off against QPR in the 1-0 loss in October 2011?
Didier Drogba

5) Thibaut Courtois was sent off during the 2-2 draw with which team in August 2015?
Swansea City

6) Which winger was sent off against West Brom in March 2006?
Arjen Robben

7) Chelsea lost 1-0 away to Aston Villa in March 2014, which two Chelsea players were dismissed?
Willian and Ramires

8) Chelsea lost a tempestuous encounter with Manchester City in February 2010, which two Chelsea players were sent off as they went down to a 4-2 defeat?
Juliano Belletti and Michael Ballack

9) Branislav Ivanovic and Fernando Torres were both sent off in a 3-2 defeat to which side in October 2012?
Manchester United

10) Frank Lampard was sent off for a foul on which Liverpool player in the February 2009 match between the two sides?
Xabi Alonso

11) Jimmy-Floyd Hasselbaink was sent off against which team in September 2001, later seeing the red card rescinded?
Arsenal

12) Chelsea and Aston Villa played a thrilling match on Boxing day 2007 in which Ricardo Carvalho and Ashley Cole saw red, but what was the final score?
4-4

13) Chelsea beat Norwich on penalties in the FA Cup in 2018 despite having which two players sent off in extra time?
Pedro and Alvaro Morata

Memorable Goals Answers

1) Who scored a stunning volley against West Ham in August 2000 after juggling the ball with his right foot and knee?
Mario Stanic

2) Who scored a spectacular overhead kick versus Leeds United in January 2003?
Eidur Gudjohnsen

3) Didier Drogba won the Premier League goal of the month in October 2009 by rounding off a stunning team move versus which side?
Bolton Wanderers

4) Who was the unlikely winner of the Premier League goal of the month in January 2010 for his turn and finish versus Sunderland?
Ashley Cole

5) In what year did Michael Essien score a stunning long-range effort with the outside of his boot to secure a 1-1 draw with Arsenal?

2006

6) Alex smashed in a long-range free kick against Arsenal in October 2010, who was in goal for the gunners?

Lukasz Fabianski

7) Who scored the equaliser against Tottenham in May 2016 to end their title hopes and hand the Premier League title to Leicester City?

Eden Hazard

8) Chelsea drew 2-2 away against Barcelona to secure a place in the 2012 Champions League Final, who scored the first goal for the Blues on the night with a deft chip?

Ramires

9) Who was in goal for Chelsea when Frank Lampard scored against his former side for Manchester City in September 2014?
Thibaut Courtois

10) Which midfielder stunned Old Trafford with a dipping effort from long-range against Manchester United in May 2005?
Thiago

11) Who scored a winner deep into injury times to secure an opening day win against newly promoted Wigan Athletic in August 2005?
Hernan Crespo

12) Claude Makelele scored his first Chelsea goal by converting a rebound from a missed penalty against which team in 2005?
Charlton Athletic

13) Who scored the winning goal against Liverpool in 2003 to seal Champions League qualification?
Jesper Gronkjaer

14) Against which team did Frank Lampard score the goal to make him Chelsea's leading goal-scorer of all time?
Aston Villa

Memorable Games Answers

1) What was the score in Frank Lampard's first game as Chelsea manager, away to Manchester United in August 2019?
4-0 to Manchester United

2) Who scored the winner in Jose Mourinho's first Premier League game as manager against Manchester United in August 2004?
Eidur Gudjohnsen

3) Arsenal faced Chelsea in Arsene Wenger's 1000th game as manager, what was the score?
Chelsea 6-0 Arsenal

4) Who scored four goals as Chelsea beat Derby County 6-1 in March 2008?
Frank Lampard

5) Who was Chelsea manager when they thrashed Aston Villa 8-0 in December 2012?
Rafael Benitez

6) Chelsea sealed the league title by tearing Wigan apart in an 8-0 win in May 2010, who was in goal for Wigan that day?
Mike Pollitt

7) Manchester City beat Chelsea 6-0 in February 2019, who scored a hat-trick in the match?
Sergio Aguero

8) What was the score-line when Chelsea beat Manchester City at home in the Premier League in October 2007?
6-0

9) Who made a superb last-minute save to claim a point for Chelsea during the dramatic 4-4 draw with Spurs in March 2008?
Carlo Cudicini

10) Which two players scored in the last 10 minutes to secure a 2-1 win away to Arsenal in December 2019?
Jorginho and Tammy Abraham

11) Chelsea sealed the Premier League title with a 2-0 away win against which side in April 2005?
Bolton Wanderers

Transfers II Answers

1) From where was Romelu Lukaku bought in 2011?
Anderlecht

2) Who did Chelsea buy from Lille in June 2012?
Eden Hazard

3) Which player did Chelsea sign from Wigan Athletic in August 2012?
Victor Moses

4) Which goalkeeper was signed from Fulham in 2013?
Mark Schwarzer

5) Which attacker was purchased from Basel in January 2014?
Mohamed Salah

6) Chelsea sold which midfielder to Wolfsburg in January 2014?
Kevin de Bruyne

7) Which two players were bought from Atletico Madrid in July 2014?
Diego Costa and Filipe Luis

8) Didier Drogba re-signed for the club from where in 2014?
Galatasaray

9) Which left back was sold to Sunderland in July 2014?
Patrick Van Aanholt

10) Chelsea sold which midfield player to Southampton in August 2015?
Oriol Romeu

11) Which defender was bought from Fiorentina in August 2016?
Marcos Alonso

12) Goalkeeper Asmir Begovic was sold to which English team in 2017?
Bournemouth

13) Which former Premier League winning midfielder arrived from Leicester City in August 2017?
Danny Drinkwater

14) Which club did John Terry sign for after leaving Chelsea in 2017?
Aston Villa

15) Striker Diego Costa was sold to which club in 2017?
Atletico Madrid

16) Which former England goalkeeper signed for Chelsea in July 2018?
Rob Green

17) Jorginho was purchased from which club in July 2018?
Napoli

18) Which team did Cesc Fabregas sign for in January 2019?
Monaco

19) Mateo Kovacic arrived from which club in July 2019?
Real Madrid

20) Which defender signed for Crystal Palace after leaving Chelsea in 2019?
Gary Cahill

Cup Games Answers

1) Who scored from the penalty spot when Chelsea beat Manchester United 1-0 in the 2018 FA Cup Final?
Eden Hazard

2) Who infamously refused to be substituted during the 2019 League Cup Final?
Kepa Arrizabalaga

3) Which lower league side beat Chelsea in the FA Cup fourth round in 2015?
Bradford City

4) How many FA cups did Ashley Cole win at Chelsea?
Four

5) Who scored twice for Chelsea as they defeated Arsenal 2-1 in the 2007 League Cup Final?
Didier Drogba

6) Chelsea beat Everton 2-1 in the 2009 FA Cup Final, but who had put Everton ahead in the first minute?
Louis Saha

7) In the FA Cup Semi Final against Newcastle in the year 2000, which player scored twice in the 2-1 win?
Gus Poyet

8) Chelsea won the last ever FA Cup Final to be staged at the old Wembley stadium in the year 2000, who scored the only goal as they defeated Aston Villa?
Roberto Di Matteo

9) Which team beat Chelsea in the FA Cup in 2001, 2002, 2003 and 2004?
Arsenal

10) Who scored the winner in extra time to win the FA Cup for Chelsea versus Manchester United in 2007?
Didier Drogba

11) Chelsea beat Liverpool 3-2 after extra time to claim the 2005 League Cup trophy, which Liverpool player scored an own goal during normal time to equalise for the blues?
Steven Gerrard

12) Which team did Chelsea hammer 7-0 in the Fa Cup third round in January 2011?
Ipswich Town

First Goals II Answers

1) Diego Costa
   Burnley

2) Joe Cole
   Notts County

3) Scott Parker
   Portsmouth

4) David Luiz
   Manchester United

5) Loic Remy
   Swansea City

6) Michael Essien
   Tottenham Hotspur

7) Deco
   Portsmouth

8) Willian
   Norwich City

9) Samuel Eto'o
   Cardiff City

10) Eden Hazard
    Newcastle United

11) Demba Ba
    Southampton

12) Mason Mount
    Leicester City

13) Tammy Abraham
    Norwich City

European Games Answers

1) Chelsea beat Bayern Munich on penalties to win the Champions League Final in 2012, but who missed Chelsea's first spot kick in the shootout?
Juan Mata

2) Who scored in stoppage time for Barcelona during the highly controversial Semi Final to knock Chelsea out of the Champions League in 2009?
Andres Iniesta

3) Who scored the late winner as Chelsea knocked Arsenal out of the Champions League at the Quarter Final stage in 2004?
Wayne Bridge

4) Which team did Chelsea lose to on penalties in the 2019 Super Cup after drawing 2-2 in normal time?
Liverpool

5) Chelsea knocked Liverpool out of the Champions League at the Quarter Final stage in 2009, but what was the aggregate score?

7-5

6) Who scored a late own goal as Liverpool drew 1-1 with Chelsea in the first leg of the Champions League Semi Final in 2008?

Jon Arne Riise

7) Who missed Chelsea's last penalty in the 2008 Champions League Final shoot-out to hand Manchester United the title?

Nicolas Anelka

8) When Chelsea faced Ajax in the group stage of the Champions League in November 2019 the Dutch side were reduced to 9 men, but what was the final score?

4-4

9) Which Chelsea player was sent off in the 2008 Champions League Final defeat to Manchester United?
Didier Drogba

10) Which team beat Chelsea in the Champions League Semi Final in 2004?
Monaco

11) Who scored the injury time winner for Chelsea in the 2013 Europa League Final versus Benfica?
Branislav Ivanovic

12) Which Swiss side knocked Chelsea out of the UEFA Cup at the First-Round stage in September 2000?
St Gallen

13) Chelsea lost in the UEFA Super Cup three times in the first 20 years of this century, which teams did they lose to?
Atletico Madrid, Bayern Munich and Liverpool

Printed in Great Britain
by Amazon

35310170R00036